It is *Written*
A Book of Bible-Based Declarations

Carlnika Hooks

Purpose Publishing

Copyright © 2021 Carlnika Hooks

All rights reserved solely by the author. The author guarantees all contents are original and do not infringe upon the legal rights of any other person or work. No part of this book may be reproduced, distributed, or transmitted in any form or by any means, or stored in a database or retrieval system, without the prior written permission of the author. The views expressed in this book are not necessarily those of the publisher.

All Scripture quotations, unless otherwise indicated, are taken from the Holy Bible, New International Version®, NIV®. Copyright ©1973, 1978, 1984, 2011 by Biblica, Inc.™ Used by permission of Zondervan. All rights reserved worldwide. www.zondervan.com The "NIV" and "New International Version" are trademarks registered in the United States Patent and Trademark Office by Biblica, Inc.™

Scripture taken from the New King James Version®. Copyright © 1982 by Thomas Nelson. Used by permission. All rights reserved.

Scripture quotations marked (ESV) are from The ESV® Bible (The Holy Bible, English Standard Version®), copyright © 2001 by Crossway, a publishing ministry of Good News Publishers. Used by permission. All rights reserved.

Scriptures marked KJV are taken from the King James Version of the Bible.

Scripture quotations taken from the (NASB®) New American Standard Bible®, Copyright © 1960, 1971, 1977, 1995, 2020 by The Lockman Foundation. Used by permission. All rights reserved. www.lockman.org

Author photo by Jacobi Bryant.

Printed in the United States of America.

ISBN: 1-955755-00-9
ISBN-13: 978-1-955755-00-9

To the Body of Christ.
May we all stand and declare
God's Word over ourselves.

CONTENTS

Introduction	1
For Repentance	5
For Overcoming the Lust of the Flesh	9
For Abiding in Jesus	15
For Physical Healing	19
For Healthy Grieving	25
For Forgiving Quickly	29
For Boldness and Courage	35
For Perseverance	41
For Victory	47
For Taking Land	53
For Being Overtaken with Joy	59
For Raising Kingdom Children	63
For Unmerited Favor	69
For Single Women in Waiting	75
For Waiting on the Lord	81
For Entrepreneurs	85
For Peace	89
For Keen Discernment	95
For Declaring the Blood of Jesus	99
For the Consuming Fire of God to Overtake You	103

Introduction

In July 2021, I started to sense in my spirit the Father wanted me to write another book. However, I had no clue on what. I shelved the thought and moved forward. Maybe a week later, a friend who operates in the gift of prophecy sensed the same thing for me. The following week I received another prophecy spoken over me that was in the same manner as the original prophecy. I began to pray into it, because at this point, I sensed an urgency in my spirit to get started. With no topic or title, I felt stuck. I juggled around some titles but did not have total peace about any of them. One day, it was like a light bulb came on. I instantly knew the Father wanted me to write another prayer book. He revealed to me the urgent need for prayer not only in this hour, but for the seasons to come.

One night my friend, Keidra Hobley, sent me a link to a live Bible study at her church. As I listened, something she would say caught my undivided attention. She started to share about Jesus and the temptation He had undergone in the wilderness by Satan. As she continued, another lightbulb came on when she said, "Jesus defeated Satan with *It is Written.*" He defeated Satan with the Word. Instantly I knew *It Is Written* would be the title to this book.

Hebrews 4:12 says, "For the word of God is alive and active. Sharper than any double-edged sword, it penetrates even to dividing soul and spirit, joints and marrow; it judges the thoughts and attitudes of the heart."

If Jesus defeated Satan with the Word, so can we. Jesus is an example for us all. He left a strategic battle plan book here for us to glean from. It is called The Bible. It is full of the Word of God.

With His words God created the heavens, the earth, every plant, every sea creature, every beast of the field, every bird, every creeping creature, and the list goes on. This reveals the power in what we say. Proverbs 18:21 says, "The tongue has the power of life and death, and those who love it will eat its fruit."

Do you see the power in that? We have the ability to speak a thing in faith and watch it come to pass. The key word here is faith. Hebrews 11:1 says, "Now faith is the substance of things hoped for, the evidence of things not seen."

It is extremely important we catch this. Faith has nothing to do with what you can see in the natural. It has everything to do with putting your hope and trust in what the Father spoke through His Word – in which you cannot see. It is believing He is not a man that He should lie, and that His word will never return to Him void. Never!

This book is full of word-based prayers with passages from me and scripture references to follow. I am more than sure you will be encouraged after professing the Word over your life and circumstances.

For Repentance

I believe before we enter into a place of prayer, we should acknowledge our sins and repent. The Father has a way of showing me my sin when I come before Him. It's like I have a hard time entering His presence when there are matters of the heart that need to be addressed. I feel strongly that those things can hinder my prayers from being answered.

I remember having a dream where the Father revealed that the sin in the hearts and lives of His people was causing their blessings to be delayed. He also revealed a spirit of witchcraft was sent to bring confusion to their minds to keep them from knowing the truth and their need for repentance. No good thing will the Father withhold from you. He would love nothing more than for you to enter the finish work of the cross to receive all He has for you, but you must do your part.

Early on in my walk with the Lord, someone introduced me to Psalm 51. It was life changing for me. I watched the words of that passage come alive in my life. Hebrews 4:12 says, "For the word of God is alive and active. Sharper than any double-edged sword, it penetrates even to dividing soul and spirit, joints and marrow; it judges the thoughts and attitudes of the heart." I had no clue what I was praying, but that did not stop the words that were alive and active from going and doing what they were sent to do.

My mindset began to change, and my actions began to line up with what was in my heart. I wanted to change but did not know how. Not only did Psalm 51 lead me into repentance, but it help manifest a lifestyle that I continue to walk in today. A holy and righteous lifestyle. Are you ready to repent?

Remember...

How did Jesus defeat Satan?

"FOR IT IS WRITTEN."

"So shall My word be that goes forth from My mouth; It shall not return to Me void, But it shall accomplish what I please, And it shall prosper in the thing for which I sent it." Isaiah 55:11 NKJV

Prayer Declaration

Have mercy on me, O God, according to your unfailing love; according to your great compassion blot out my transgressions. Wash away all my iniquity and cleanse me from my sin. For I know my transgressions, and my sin is always before me. Against you, you only, have I sinned and done what is evil in your sight; so you are right in your verdict and justified when you judge. Surely I was sinful at birth, sinful from the time my mother conceived me. Yet you desired faithfulness even in the womb; you taught me wisdom in that secret place. Cleanse me with hyssop, and I will be clean; wash me, and I will be whiter than snow. Let me hear joy and gladness; let the bones you have crushed rejoice. Hide your face from my sins and blot out all my iniquity. Create in me a pure heart, O God, and renew a steadfast spirit within me. Do not cast me from your presence or take your Holy Spirit from me. Restore to me the joy of your salvation and grant me a willing spirit, to sustain me. Then I will teach transgressors your ways, so that sinners will turn back to you. Open my lips, Lord, and my mouth will declare your praise. You do not delight in sacrifice, or I would bring it; you do not take pleasure in burnt offerings. My sacrifice, O God, is a broken spirit; a broken and contrite heart you, God, will not despise (Psalm 51:1-12, 15-17). In Jesus' Name, amen.

For Overcoming the Lust of the Flesh

Overcoming lust was a struggle for me. I was molested at the age of five by my sixteen-year-old cousin who just so happen to be a girl. In that moment, doors were opened that were not shut until my late twenties. I struggled with perversion, and I had a serious identity crisis.

I wanted to desperately escape the lusting spirit that had its grip on me, but I did not know how. After I gave my life to Christ, I found myself falling back into the same sexual sin the Father had delivered me out of. This was definitely the sin that easily beset me.

I started to notice a pattern. In that, the Father would begin to show me what steps to take to completely go free. For whom the Son sets free, is free indeed. He began to show me practical steps. I stopped drinking. I noticed every time I drank, I would find myself in bed with a man. It was like drinking triggered the lusting demon in me and caused me to lose all self-control. Not watching movies that had sexual sensation was another practical step I took. Deliverance was a part of the process, but the ultimate step was an effective prayer declaration. I had to believe the Father would meet me right where I was.

It was two years before I finally went totally free from that sin. The Father was loving, gracious, and patient in that season. I never premeditated sin but would continually fall into it by not taking these practical steps. I remember waking up the next day drowning myself in tears because I felt so dirty. I remember the day I woke up and it was like I knew I would never go back to that sin. Something happened. That last time I fell was the only time I did not cry. I walked away with a feeling of assurance that I was free. Weird, I know. I'm a decade into freedom from that sin. My mind and heart are made up. Yours can be too. Are you ready to overcome the lust of the flesh?

Remember…

How did Jesus defeat Satan?

"FOR IT IS WRITTEN."

"So shall My word be that goes forth from My mouth; It shall not return to Me void, But it shall accomplish what I please, And it shall prosper in the thing for which I sent it." Isaiah 55:11 NKJV

Prayer Declaration

I declare I am fleeing all youthful lusts and following righteousness, faith, love, and peace. I will call on the Father with a pure heart. I declare that Jesus has made me free and I am free indeed. I declare that I belong to Jesus, and because of that my flesh, with its affections and lusts, have been crucified. I declare I am born of God and as a result I will not go on sinning. I declare I am being cleansed from all filthiness of the flesh and spirit. Holiness is being perfected in me because I have the fear of God in my heart. I declare I am more than a conqueror. I will walk in the Spirit, and I will not fulfill the lust of my flesh. I declare I will stand fast in the liberty where with Jesus has made me free. I will not be entangled again with the yoke of bondage. I declare I will set no evil thing before my eyes. I hate the work of them that turn aside. It shall not cleave to me. In Jesus' Name, amen.

Scripture References

"Flee also youthful lusts; but pursue righteousness, faith, love, peace with those who call on the Lord out of a pure heart." 2 Timothy 2:22 NKJV

"So if the Son sets you free, you will be free indeed." John 8:36 NIV

"Those who belong to Christ Jesus have crucified the flesh with its passions and desires." Galatians 5:24 NIV

"No one who is born of God will continue to sin, because God's seed remains in them; they cannot go on sinning, because they have been born of God." 1 John 3:9 NIV

"Therefore, having these promises, beloved, let us cleanse ourselves from all filthiness of the flesh and spirit, perfecting holiness in the fear of God." 2 Corinthians 7:1 NKJV

"No, in all these things we are more than conquerors through him who loved us." Romans 8:37 NIV

"I say then: Walk in the Spirit, and you shall not fulfill the lust of the flesh." Galatians 5:16 NKJV

"Stand fast therefore in the liberty by which Christ has made us free, and do not be entangled again with a yoke of bondage." Galatians 5:1 NKJV

"I will set nothing wicked before my eyes; I hate the work of those who fall away; It shall not cling to me."
Psalms 101:3 NKJV

For Abiding in Jesus

I believe with everything in me abiding in Jesus is by far the most important thing you can do. The word abide means to live, dwell, remain, stay, or reside. When I look at the definition, it is clear to me. We should remain in Christ. We should never venture out from the place we should dwell.

I have noticed in my own life anytime I begin to feel fear, unrest, no peace, or anxious, I have somehow ventured away from the place that should be my resting place. This place can only be found in Jesus.

Abiding in Jesus gives me peace beyond my circumstances. Abiding in Jesus gives me rest in my spirit in the mist of a storm. Abiding in Jesus gives me an assurance that no matter what I face I come out on the other side victorious. Abiding in Jesus is where I am fully aware that I am valued and loved. Abiding in Jesus is where every lie is exposed, and the truth is revealed. Abiding in Jesus is where I know I am safe. Abiding in Jesus is where you will find the answer to a problem or question you've been having.

I remember having a vision of me walking into Jesus' body and taking a seat. I felt this overwhelming sense of peace. I began to weep. I felt so loved and protected. Nothing I was up against mattered anymore.

If we could learn how to be still and abide in Jesus even in the busiest times of our lives, life would go such much smoother. Less depression diagnoses. Less anger. Less feelings of anxiousness. Less fear. Less feelings of inadequacy. I know without a shadow of a doubt the numbers to any physical diagnoses made in our physical health as well as our emotional health would go down.

A lot of what we face in our emotions has everything to do with not taking out intentional time to be with the Lord. I know life can get busy, but I also know we can make time for we want to make time for. Get up early or go to sleep late. Whatever you need to do for a healthier you, should be done.

Abiding in Jesus is essential. The word essential means

absolutely necessary and extremely important. It is extremely important that you understand it is absolutely necessary for you to make time to abide in Jesus. Are you ready to abide in Him?

Remember…

How did Jesus defeat Satan?

"FOR IT IS WRITTEN."

"So shall My word be that goes forth from My mouth; It shall not return to Me void, But it shall accomplish what I please, And it shall prosper in the thing for which I sent it." Isaiah 55:11 NKJV

Prayer Declaration

Father teach me how to abide in You that I may bear fruit, because apart from You I can do nothing. Let the fruit I obtain from abiding in You bring You glory. In this shall it be proven that I am Your disciple. Father, in You is where I find safety and know that I am loved. May love, joy, peace, patience, kindness, goodness, faithfulness, gentleness, and self-control be my portion as a result of me abiding in You. I will walk in the same manner as You because I choose to abide in You. As I abide in You, my strength will be renewed and hope will be restored. In Jesus' Name, amen.

Scripture References

"Abide in Me, and I in you. As the branch cannot bear fruit of itself, unless it abides in the vine, neither can you, unless you abide in Me." John 15:4 NKJV

"I am the vine, you are the branches. He who abides in Me, and I in him, bears much fruit; for without Me you can do nothing." John 15:5 NKJV

"This is to my Father's glory, that you bear much fruit, showing yourselves to be my disciples." John 15:8 NIV

"But the fruit of the Spirit is love, joy, peace, forbearance, kindness, goodness, faithfulness, gentleness and self-control." Galatians 5:22-23 NIV

"He who says he abides in Him ought himself also to walk just as He walked." 1 John 2:6 NKJV

"But those who hope in the Lord will renew their strength." Isaiah 40:31

For Physical Healing

Jesus is the same yesterday, today, and forever. Do you believe that? When Jesus walked the earth as a man, there was not one person He came across that believed by faith that He could heal them, that was not healed. Everyone who believed He could heal, received it. In Matthew 8:2, a man with leprosy asked Jesus if He was willing to heal him. Jesus answered, "I'm willing." I believe the same applies to us today.

There are different factors that can play a part in us receiving our healing. For example, when the Father gives you instructions, please follow them. If He tells you to go roll in a puddle of mud, go roll in a puddle of mud. There are different examples all throughout the Bible where instructions were given in order for someone to receive their healing. Think about Naaman, the man with the leprosy. Elisha told him to go get in the Jordan River and wash seven times so that he may receive his healing. Naaman was furious. He did not want to go do such a thing. The Jordan was known for being unclean water. He wondered why Elisha could not come down himself to bring healing to his body. Why go through all the extra? The extra was the instruction Elisha received from the Lord. It is a possibility Naaman was full of pride and this may have been a way for him to walk in humility. You never know, but what I do know is that we should obey the instructions of the Lord.

The Father may not give you specific instruction. Your case may be the timing – the waiting process between the time you first prayed to the time your healing manifests. It may take years, or it may take days. However long it takes, remember who Your Father is. Jehovah Rapha, the Lord heals. Are you ready to be healed?

Remember…

How did Jesus defeat Satan?

"FOR IT IS WRITTEN."

"So shall My word be that goes forth from My mouth; It shall not return to Me void, But it shall accomplish what I please, And it shall prosper in the thing for which I sent it." Isaiah 55:11 NKJV

Prayer Declaration

Father Your word says in Galatians 3:13, You redeemed me from the curse of the law and became the curse for me. Heal me, O Lord, and I will be healed. Save me and I will be saved. You are the One I praise. I will not fear for You are with me. I will not be dismayed for You are my God. Thank You for strengthening me and helping me. Thank You for upholding me with Your righteous right hand. I declare Jeremiah 30:17. You are restoring my health and healing my wounds. Thank You for restoring me physically and emotionally. Father You were pierced for my transgressions. You were crushed for my iniquities. The punishment that brought me peace was on You, and by the thirty-nine stripes You took on my behalf I am healed! Thank You for restoring me to health and letting me live according to Isaiah 38:16. I declare You have brought health and healing to me. I will enjoy abundant peace and security. I declare I will enjoy good health, and all will go well with me, even as my soul prospers. In Jesus' Name, amen.

Scripture References

"Christ redeemed us from the curse of the law by becoming a curse for us, for it is written: "Cursed is everyone who is hung on a pole." Galatians 3:13 NIV

"Heal me, LORD, and I will be healed; save me and I will be saved, for you are the one I praise." Jeremiah 17:14 NIV

"So do not fear, for I am with you; do not be dismayed, for I am your God. I will strengthen you and help you; I will uphold you with my righteous right hand." Isaiah 40:10 NIV

"But I will restore you to health and heal your wounds,' declares the LORD, 'because you are called an outcast, Zion for whom no one cares." Jeremiah 30:17 NIV

"But he was pierced for our transgressions, he was crushed for our iniquities; the punishment that brought us peace was on him, and by his wounds we are healed." Isaiah 53:5 NIV

"Lord, by such things people live; and my spirit finds life in them too. You restored me to health and let me live." Isaiah 38:16 NIV

"Nevertheless, I will bring health and healing to it; I will heal my people and will let them enjoy abundant peace and security." Jeremiah 33:6 NIV

"Dear friend, I pray that you may enjoy good health and that all may go well with you, even as your soul is getting along well." 3 John 1:2 NIV

For Healthy Grieving

I know all too well about unhealthy and healthy grieving. I've had a great deal of loss of loved ones in my life. My son's father was murdered, my dad passed from lung cancer, and the list continues. My dad and my son's father were the ones that hurt the most.

The grief I experienced from both incidents were different. I grieved in a healthy way with my son's father, but with my dad, not so much. With my son's father, the Word carried me through. Taking the time out to process my way through my feelings was a huge factor. I had my moments where I would just cry. It seemed as if it would be the same day around the same time, but the grieving was healthy. I was hurt but not depressed. I had hope that we could continue, and that God would be a father to my son.

My dad's passing and the way I handled it was entirely different. I was hopeless and did not see the need to continue on. I could not believe these were my thoughts. I was in a dark place. There were no words that anyone could have expressed to make me feel better. I did not want company or to be in the presence of anyone. When people would ask me how they could help I would tell them, "Just pray." I knew that was the only thing that would pull me out of the pit of despair and darkness. I remember calling on the name of Jesus because that was all I had. By the third day he resurrected me. I could see the light at the end of the tunnel. I felt like I could continue on. I was hopeful. I then began to grieve in a very different way – a healthy way.

The loss of a loved one, or anything that brings grief, can be life-altering. It is extremely important that we grieve in a healthy way. I came out in three days, but there are others that stay in a dark place for years. We get angry with God and begin to blame Him for the outcome. We turn our backs on Him instead of running to Him. He loves you and He knows what it feels like to lose someone.

Let me encourage you. There is hope in Jesus Christ during the storm and in the midst of you questioning why. I had my days where I wanted to know why. The Father is faithful enough to show you exactly why. He did it for me, and He can do it for you. Are you ready to grieve in a healthy way?

Remember…

How did Jesus defeat Satan?

"FOR IT IS WRITTEN."

"So shall My word be that goes forth from My mouth; It shall not return to Me void, But it shall accomplish what I please, And it shall prosper in the thing for which I sent it." Isaiah 55:11 NKJV

Prayer Declaration

Father, Your grace is sufficient for me. Your power is made perfect in my weakness. Your word says, You are close to the brokenhearted. Heal my heart and restore hope to me. Mend back the broken pieces that I may grieve in a healthy way. You are my stronghold in times of trouble. You are my Rock and my Deliverer in whom I take refuge in. You are my shield and the horn of my salvation. Father I thank You that You save those who are crushed in spirit. I declare You are healing my broken heart and binding up my wounds. I give You all my worries for You care for me. I declare the joy of the Lord is my strength. I will rest in knowing all things work together for the good of them that love You and are called according to Your purpose. In Jesus name, amen.

Scripture References

And He has said to me, "My grace is sufficient for you, for power is perfected in weakness." 1 Corinthians 12:9 KJV

"The LORD is a refuge for the oppressed, a stronghold in times of trouble." Psalm 9:9 NIV

"The LORD is my rock, and my fortress, and my deliverer; my God, my strength, in whom I will trust; my buckler, and the horn of my salvation, and my high tower."
Psalm 21:1 NIV

"He heals the brokenhearted and binds up their wounds." Psalm 147:3 NIV

"Nehemiah said, "Go and enjoy choice food and sweet drinks, and send some to those who have nothing prepared. This day is holy to our LORD. Do not grieve, for the joy of the LORD is your strength." Nehemiah 8:10 NIV

"And we know that all things work together for good to them that love God, to them who are the called according to his purpose." Romans 8:28 KJV

FOR FORGIVING QUICKLY

The word forgive means to stop feeling angry or resentful toward someone for an offense, flaw, or mistake. As I began to prepare to write this excerpt, the first thing I heard was, "Forgiveness means to not keep a record of wrongs." Immediately, I was reminded of 1 Corinthians 13:5. Holding an offense towards someone does not hurt them, but indeed it hurts you. Forgiving someone is normally not for the other person, but for you.

I remember getting really sick in my body. I had no clue what was wrong with me. I felt like my organs was shutting down. I could barely breathe. I had little strength to move around. A prophet reached out to me and said, "That which you are sick with will pass through your bowels." The next day nothing. I was just as sick as I was the day before. I got up to go to the restroom. As I sat there this still small voice said, "Forgive her." I knew exactly who the voice was referring to. As soon as I cried out and said, "I forgive her," my bowels moved and I was instantly healed.

I was holding on to something that caused an infection to set up in my body. Unforgiveness can be toxic for you, not the other person. While they are moving on with their life, you are suffering with the torment of what they did to you.

Forgiveness is a choice. You can choose to forgive as soon as the offense occurs. The part that can be a little discomforting is the process – the process between the moment you chose to forgive to the moment the forgiveness actually manifests in your mind and heart. This is where the Word comes in.

I remember being hurt by several Christians all at once. I was being accused of things I did not do. It was the word of God that allowed me to walk in love and truly pray for those people rather than curse them. In that season of my life, I had a newfound respect for the Word of God because I knew there was no way I could love those people on my own.

Forgiveness is a requirement. Jesus was very adamant about that. "For if you forgive other people when they sin against you, your heavenly Father will also forgive you.

But if do not forgive others their sins, your Father will not forgive your sins." (Matthew 6:14-15 NIV) Will you choose to forgive for your sake?

Remember…

How did Jesus defeat Satan?

"FOR IT IS WRITTEN."

"So shall My word be that goes forth from My mouth; It shall not return to Me void, But it shall accomplish what I please, And it shall prosper in the thing for which I sent it." Isaiah 55:11 NKJV

Prayer Declaration

Father, I choose to forgive [names]. Your Word says that Your love is shed abroad in my heart. I'm thankful Your love gives me the ability to love in a selfless way. I will not keep a record of wrongs. I choose to forgive quickly. I rebuke every word whispering in my ears telling me to hold on to an offense. I silence the voice of the enemy by choosing to not only walk in love, but to bless and pray for those who have hurt me. I listen to the voice of the Lord and the voice of a stranger I will not follow. The Word of God says to forgive seventy times seven a day. I declare I shall forgive as often as an offense occurs. Peace be still in my mind and in my heart. I am patient. I am kind. I will not be easily angered or easily offended. For You, oh God, dwell in my heart and for that I am rooted and grounded in the love. In Jesus' Name, amen.

Scripture References

"And hope maketh not ashamed; because the love of God is shed abroad in our hearts by the Holy Ghost." Romans 5:5 NKJV

"That Christ may dwell in your hearts by faith; that ye, being rooted and grounded in love." Ephesian 3:17 NKJV

"It does not dishonor others, it is not self-seeking, it is not easily angered, it keeps no record of wrongs." 1 Corinthians 13:5 NIV

"My sheep hear my voice, and I know them, and they follow me." John 10:27 KJV

Jesus answered, "I tell you, not seven times, but seventy-seven times. Matthew 18:22 NIV

"But I tell you, love your enemies and pray for those who persecute you." Matthew 5:44 NIV

"Then He arose and rebuked the wind, and said to the sea, "Peace, be still!" And the wind ceased and there was a great calm." Mark 4:39 NKJV

"Love is patient, love is kind." 1 Corinthians 13:4 NIV

For Boldness and Courage

Every season we enter we should ask for a new level of boldness. Each season we encounter a new level of warfare. The greater the assignment, the greater the push back. You must be prepared mentally and physically, because if not, there is a huge chance you will quit. You will raise your white flag of surrender.

I am always reminded of Joshua, Caleb, and the ten spies. Two believe they could take the land promised by God, and ten did not. The ten allowed the giants on the land to intimidate them into believing the promise was unachievable. The ten allowed the size of the giants and the voice of the enemy saying, "You cannot win," to speak louder than the voice of God. Whose voice will you believe?

In Joshua chapter one, God told Joshua four times to be strong and courageous. The third time He added the word *command*. He said, "Have I not commanded you? Be strong and courageous." (Joshua 1:9a NIV)

The Father knew there were things they were about to face that if not rooted in the truth they could possibly coward down and forfeit the promise. The truth is simple. They have the victory in Christ Jesus, and what the Father promised belongs to them.

The word *command* means to give an authoritative order. Charge, demand, and decree are words that best describes the word *command*. The words *bold* and *courageous* are one in the same, but we will take a closer look at the word *bold*.

Bold means to show an ability to take risks. Courageous, brave, valiant, fearless, dauntless, unafraid, and confident are all words that describe the word *bold*.

Last but not least, the word *strong* means to withstand great force or pressure. Well-built, durable, indestructible, solid, well-made, long-lasting, and enduring are all words that describe the word *strong*.

I believe the Father is giving us the same charge He gave Joshua as we approach the end times. It takes a certain level of boldness to stand in the face of our adversaries. The Father would never tell us to be strong and courageous if He knew we would not have the victory in the end. He knows our ending from our beginning and all things in between. However, we do not. We see in part. We see only what He allows us to. Even in that it is always enough to believe what seems impossible is actually possible. For we know what is impossible with man is possible with God.

Will you choose to stand and face the giants in the land that stand between you and your promise? Will you stand and not bow like Shadrach, Meshach, and Abednego knowing it is a huge chance you will be thrown into the fiery furnace? Will you worship, pray, and praise God like Daniel did in the face of your enemies who have the power to throw you in the lion's den?

Remember...

How did Jesus defeat Satan?

"FOR IT IS WRITTEN."

"So shall My word be that goes forth from My mouth; It shall not return to Me void, But it shall accomplish what I please, And it shall prosper in the thing for which I sent it." Isaiah 55:11 NKJV

Prayer Declaration

Father I come in the Name of Jesus asking that You endow me with a new level of boldness for this new season I am entering. Give me the ability to stand up against my enemies the way Daniel, Shadrach, Meshach, Abednego, David, Joshua, and Caleb did. Let the lion within me roar louder than the voices in my ear telling me to retreat. I will be strong and courageous! I will fight! I will stand and I will win! I will not be afraid or terrified of my enemies, because You go with me. You will never leave me nor forsake me. Yea though I walk through the valley of the shadow of death I will not fear for You are with me. I will not be discouraged because You go with me. I will be on my guard and I will stand firm in my faith. My Father will not fail me nor will He forsake me. I will be strong and take heart because all my hope is in the Lord. I will be strengthened, and the Father will help me. He will uphold me with His righteous right hand. For God has not given me a spirit of fear, but of power, love, and a sound mind. I declare I am well built. I am durable. I am indestructible. I am well made by my Creator! I am built to last long, and I shall endure to the end! I declare I am brave, valiant, fearless, dauntless, unafraid, and confident in the mighty and matchless Name of Jesus Christ, amen!

Scripture References

"Be strong and courageous. Do not be afraid or terrified because of them, for the Lord your God goes with you; he will never leave you nor forsake you." Deuteronomy 31:6 NIV

"Be on your guard; stand firm in the faith; be courageous; be strong." 1 Corinthians 16:13 NIV

"David also said to Solomon his son, "Be strong and courageous, and do the work. Do not be afraid or discouraged, for the Lord God, my God, is with you. He will not fail you or forsake you until all the work for the service of the temple of the Lord is finished."
1 Chronicles 28:20 NIV

"Be strong and take heart, all you who hope in the Lord." Psalms 31:24 NIV

"So do not fear, for I am with you; do not be dismayed, for I am your God. I will strengthen you and help you; I will uphold you with my righteous right hand." Isaiah 41:10 NIV

"God has not given us a spirit of fear and timidity, but of power, love, and self-discipline." 2 Timothy 1:7 NIV

For Perseverance

I remember having a dream about being instructed to teach the next generation about perseverance. I feel so strongly that not only does the next generation need to be taught how to persevere, but so do we. The word persevere means to continue in a course of action even in the face of difficulty or with little or no prospect of success.

The last ten years of my life should be called the season of perseverance. I spent my thirties learning how to press through some of the most challenging times of my life. From the death of my son's father, to not knowing how my son and I were going to eat, to the passing of my dad. I was also homeless for a while, sleeping in my car. This is just to name a few.

I was not living a reckless life. I had given the Father a *yes* and decided I would follow Him to the ends of the earth. My faith was tested beyond measure and the enemy tempted me beyond measure. I remember having a dream where someone told me, "Satan has asked to sift you as wheat." I feel like I felt every bit of that, but I also felt the latter end of what Jesus said in Luke 22:32 – but I have prayed that your faith fail not. Tears are literally wailing up in my eyes as I type this. This journey has not been an easy one, but still a rewarding one. The rewards for me are all the souls that have come into the Kingdom on this journey, the healings that have taken place, and me walking hand-in-hand with the Lord. He has become my best friend.

This journey has taught me how to wait on God. How to seek, listen, and obey. I feel like I can press my way through anything because the Father is with me. If He sent me, He will surely take care of me. If He brings me to it, He will surely bring me through it.

I had a moment of press through in getting to the finish line for the completion of this book. Just as I finished writing and was ready to proofread, my flash drive malfunctioned, and I lost the entire book. You talk about a moment where I was ready to throw in the towel. I was so hurt, with little to no strength. I went through some serious warfare to write this book, only to have to start over from scratch. I did not remember the prayers nor the topics. As I surrendered to the Father, He woke me up in the middle of the night and gave me all the topics. They were coming so fast I could not believe it. The enemy may have a plan, but the Father has a bigger plan – a plan that will thwart the plan of the enemy.

If we do not learn to persevere, there are certain blessings we will never obtain. Perseverance produces character and character, hope. I needed all three. What good will it do for you to get the blessing or the promotion but do not have the character to sustain it.

I think about wine and how it's created – grapes in a presser being crushed. Then I question if new wine can go into old wine skin. Surely not. The old wine skin will burst. You need new wine and new wine skin. You need a new mindset for the new season. A press through season is needed to get you where you need to be so that you will steward well what the Father has for you. Are you ready to persevere?

Remember…

How did Jesus defeat Satan?

"FOR IT IS WRITTEN."

"So shall My word be that goes forth from My mouth; It shall not return to Me void, But it shall accomplish what I please, And it shall prosper in the thing for which I sent it." Isaiah 55:11 NKJV

Prayer Declaration

I come before the throne of God asking for perseverance. Perseverance, arise in me. My eyes will look directly forward and my gaze straight before me. I shall ponder the path of my feet and then all my ways shall be established. I am sure the Father will bring to completion the work He has begun in me. I will keep my face like flint, directed towards the Lord. I will press towards the goal for the prize for the upward call of God in Christ Jesus. I will hold fast to the confession of my hope without wavering, for the Father who promised is faithful. I will consider it pure joy whenever I face trials of many kinds, because I know the testing of my faith produces perseverance. Perseverance will finish its work so that I may be mature and complete, not lacking anything. I will lay aside every weight and sin that clings to me, and I will run with endurance the race that is set before me. I will remain steadfast under trial, for when I have been tested, I will receive the crown of life. I will not grow weary in well doing, for in due season I will reap. I will not give up. I will persevere. In Jesus' Name, amen.

Scripture References

"Let your eyes look directly forward, and your gaze be straight before you. Ponder the path of your feet; then all your ways will be sure." Proverbs 4:25-26 NIV

"And I am sure of this, that he who began a good work in you will bring it to completion at the day of Jesus Christ." Philippians 1:6 NIV

"Brothers, I do not consider that I have made it my own. But one thing I do: forgetting what lies behind and straining forward to what lies ahead. I press on toward the goal for the prize of the upward call of God in Christ Jesus." Philippians 3:13-14 NIV

"Let us hold fast the confession of our hope without wavering, for he who promised is faithful." Hebrews 10:23 NIV

"Count it all joy, my brothers, when you meet trials of various kinds, for you know that the testing of your faith produces steadfastness. And let steadfastness have its full effect, that you may be perfect and complete, lacking in nothing." James 1:2-4 NIV

"Blessed is the man who remains steadfast under trial, for when he has stood the test he will receive the crown of life, which God has promised to those who love him." James 1:12 NIV

"And let us not grow weary of doing good, for in due season we will reap, if we do not give up." Galatians 6:9 NIV

For Victory

There will be many times in our lives where we face opposition of some sort that screams, "You cannot win." Do you know you have victory in Jesus Christ? There has never been a battle He has not won. Even when it seems like you are about to lose, the Father has a way of turning things around for your good and His glory. All things work together for the good of them that love Jesus. All things. Not some things. All.

I have faced battle after battle, and I'm quite sure you have as well. The same God that led you into victory last time, will be the same God that leads you into victory this time.

I think about David and how he brought himself back into

remembrance of his past victories. When he faced Goliath, his faith was built in such a way where he could not be moved. He knew the same God then is the same God now. He does not change. Who is the uncircumcised Philistine that stands between you and victory? I am here to tell you there is no battle too big for God.

I think about a dream I had. I jumped off a mountain and landed on my feet. I said, "Only God could have done this." People were standing around looking. There are people standing around waiting for you to fall flat on your face, but the only thing they will witness is the victory that awaits you. The Father has a way of setting the stage where your enemies are looking on as He take you higher. Elevation you shall see.

I'm here to tell you the Father is about to pull you out of the mud and mire, and your feet will land on solid ground. Be encouraged. You shall see victory. Are you ready for victory?

Remember…

How did Jesus defeat Satan?

"FOR IT IS WRITTEN."

"So shall My word be that goes forth from My mouth; It shall not return to Me void, But it shall accomplish what I please, And it shall prosper in the thing for which I sent it." Isaiah 55:11 NKJV

Prayer Declaration

Father, thank You that You go with me to fight for me against my enemies to give me victory. Thanks be to God for You give me victory through Jesus Christ! For I am more than a conqueror in You. Thanks be to You, Father who always leads me in triumph in Christ, and through me diffuses the fragrance of Your knowledge in every place. There is no battle I cannot win for I can do all things through Christ who strengthens me. My struggle is not against flesh and blood, but against the rulers, against authorities, against the powers of this dark world, and against the spiritual forces of evil in the heavenly realms. Therefore, I will put on the full armor of God, so when the day of evil comes I may be able to stand my ground. I will stand firm with the buckle of truth wrapped around my waist, with the breastplate of righteousness in place, and with feet fitted with the readiness that comes from the gospel of peace. I will take up my shield of faith, so that I can extinguish all the flaming arrows of the evil one. I will take the helmet of salvation and the sword of the Spirit (the Word of God), so that I may be battle ready. Victory belongs to me. In Jesus' Name, amen.

Scripture References

"But thanks be to God! He gives us the victory through our Lord Jesus Christ." 1 Corinthians 15:57 NIV

"No, in all these things we are more than conquerors through him who loved us." Romans 8:37 NIV

"But thanks be to God, who always leads us as captives in Christ's triumphal procession and uses us to spread the aroma of the knowledge of him everywhere." 2 Corinthians 2:14 NIV

"I can do all this through him who gives me strength." Philippians 4:13 NIV

"Finally, be strong in the Lord and in his mighty power. Put on the full armor of God, so that you can take your stand against the devil's schemes. For our struggle is not against flesh and blood, but against the rulers, against the authorities, against the powers of this dark world and against the spiritual forces of evil in the heavenly realms. Therefore put on the full armor of God, so that when the day of evil comes, you may be able to stand your ground, and after you have done everything, to stand. Stand firm then, with the belt of truth buckled around your waist, with the breastplate of righteousness in place, and with your feet fitted with the readiness that comes from the gospel of peace. In addition to all this, take up the shield of faith, with which you can extinguish all the flaming arrows of the evil one. Take the helmet of salvation and the sword of the Spirit, which is the word of God." Ephesians 6:10-17 NIV

For Taking Land

Ten years ago, the Father started pressing upon my heart to look into purchasing land. He began to reveal to me the purpose behind His people owning their own land. He revealed we should invest in multiple places all around the world if we are called to do so.

The Father is putting His people into position just as He did for Joseph. Many will be in position to save nations, states, and cities due to the wisdom they have accumulated over the years pertaining to the marketplace. You will be in position to bless the widow and orphan, to employ those who are jobless, and give shelter to those who are homeless. He also revealed to me the significance of growing your own crops. Everything that produces something, you may want to

For Taking Land

look into it.

Not only did He show me the importance of purchasing land in the natural, but he revealed to me the importance of taking land in the spirit. This can be done through worship, prayer and praise. You go to places instructed by the Holy Spirit to uproot, tear down, and build in the spirit. You tear down altars built by Satan, and you build the Father an altar. Only go where the Father leads you. Where He leads there will be protection. Divine protection. The land you go to take in the spirit may not be the land you may own one day, but it will be land that will serve kingdom purposes owned by another. This is why it is extremely important to move at the beat of the Holy Spirit. Your obedience makes it easy for our brothers and sisters to come behind you, and take what rightfully belongs to the Kingdom of God.

I believe that every abortion mill I go to will one day be a place for life. A place of hope. My assignment is to only uproot, tear down, and build. It is someone else's assignment to actually purchase the land. It is almost like going to slay the giant before they arrive.

There may be someone occupying the land the Father has promised you, or led you to purchase. If this is the case, please remember the Father said it belongs to you. This gives you the legal right in the spirit to call forth that which He said belongs to you. Are you ready to take your land?

Remember…

How did Jesus defeat Satan?

"FOR IT IS WRITTEN."

"So shall My word be that goes forth from My mouth; It shall not return to Me void, But it shall accomplish what I please, And it shall prosper in the thing for which I sent it." Isaiah 55:11 NKJV

Prayer Declaration

Father, Your word says wherever the soles of my feet tread that land belongs to me. I declare I will take possession of the land that has been promised to me. I shall settle there. I will arise and walk through the land promised to me in the length of it and in the breadth of it, for I know my Father will give it to me. Father bless me with the blessing of Abraham that I may possess the land of my sojourning. I shall possess the land flowing with milk and honey. Every giant standing in my way shall be slain just as David slayed Goliath. I declare I will tear down all demonic altars the Father sends me to, and dash into pieces their pillars and burn them with the fire of God in the spirit. I shall uproot, tear down, and build for kingdom purposes. Father the earth is Yours and all that is in it.

Help me to steward well what You entrust to me. In Jesus' Name, amen.

Scripture References

"Every place that the sole of your foot will tread upon I have given you, as I said to Moses." Joshua 1:3 NKJV

"See, I have set the land before you; go in and possess the land which the LORD swore to your fathers to Abraham, Isaac, and Jacob to give to them and their descendants after them." Deuteronomy 1:8 NKJV

"Arise, walk in the land through its length and its width, for I give it to you." Genesis 13:17 NKJV

"May he give the blessing of Abraham to you and to your offspring with you, that you may take possession of the land of your sojournings that God gave to Abraham!" Genesis 28:4 ESV

"Hence I have said to you, "You are to possess their land, and I Myself will give it to you to possess it, a land flowing with milk and honey." I am the Lord your God, who has separated you from the peoples." Leviticus 20:24 NASB

"You shall tear down their altars and dash in pieces their pillars and burn their Asherim with fire. You shall chop down the carved images of their gods and destroy their name out of that place." Deuteronomy 12:3 ESV

"The heavens are Yours, the earth also is Yours; The world and all its fullness, You have founded them." Psalms 89:11 NKJV

For Being Overtaken with Joy

My word for the year 2021 was joy. I was so excited because the battle I had just come out of the year prior almost left my hope deferred. What I did not suspect was how I would have to claim joy as my portion, because my faith would be tested even the more so. Although there would be things ahead that would bring me joy, I first had to press my way through all the fog to enter into it.

Joy is not just for when things are going well. I learned that I can have joy no matter the circumstance. The joy of the Lord is your portion. Claim it. Are you ready to enter into joy?

Remember...

How did Jesus defeat Satan?

"FOR IT IS WRITTEN."

"So shall My word be that goes forth from My mouth; It shall not return to Me void, But it shall accomplish what I please, And it shall prosper in the thing for which I sent it." Isaiah 55:11 NKJV

Prayer Declaration

Father, You make known to me the path of life. You will fill me with joy in Your presence, with eternal pleasures at Your right hand. Even in my times of despair I will rejoice, because the joy of the Lord is my strength. I will go out in joy and be led forth in peace. I have sown in tears, and I shall surely reap in joy if I faint not. I declare the Father is giving me joy for mourning, and beauty for ashes. I shall abide in the Father where I will find strength and joy. I delight greatly in the Lord. My soul rejoices in my God. He has clothed me with garments of salvation and arrayed me in a robe of His righteousness, as a bridegroom adorns his head like a priest, and as a bride adorns herself with her jewels. My lips will shout for joy when I sing praise to You. Though the fig tree does not bud and there are no grapes on the vines, though the olive crop fails and the fields produce no food, though there are no sheep in the pen and no cattle in the stalls, yet I will rejoice in the Lord. I will be joyful in God my Savior. The sovereign Lord is my strength. He makes my feet like the feet of a deer. He enables me to tread on the heights. May the God of hope fill me with all joy and peace as I trust in Him, so that I may overflow with hope by the power of the Holy Spirit. In Jesus' Name, amen.

Scripture References

"You make known to me the path of life; you will fill me with joy in your presence, with eternal pleasures at your right hand." Psalms 16:11 NIV

"Nehemiah said, 'Go and enjoy choice food and sweet drinks, and send some to those who have nothing prepared. This day is holy to our Lord. Do not grieve, for the joy of the LORD is your strength." Nehemiah 8:10 NIV

"You will go out in joy and be led forth in peace; the mountains and hills will burst into song before you, and all the trees of the field will clap their hands."
Isaiah 55:12 NIV

"Strength and joy are in His dwelling place."
1 Chronicles 16:27 NIV

"Those who sow with tears will reap with songs of joy. Those who go out weeping, carrying seed to sow, will return with songs of joy, carrying sheaves with them."
Psalms 126:5-6 NIV

"I delight greatly in the LORD; my soul rejoices in my God. For he has clothed me with garments of salvation and arrayed me in a robe of his righteousness, as a bridegroom adorns his head like a priest, and as a bride adorns herself with her jewels." Isaiah 61:10 NIV

"Though the fig tree does not bud and there are no grapes on the vines, though the olive crop fails and the fields produce no food, though there are no sheep in the pen and no cattle in the stalls, yet I will rejoice in the LORD, I will be joyful in God my Savior. The Sovereign LORD is my strength; he makes my feet like the feet of a deer, he enables me to tread on the heights."
Habakkuk 3:17-19 NIV

For Raising Kingdom Children

The enemy has made it very clear that he is after our children. I thank God that I serve the Creator of all creation who has all power in His hands. Read that again. ALL power. Jesus defeated hell on our behalf and has given us authority here on earth to trample over the serpent, and we shall.

It is our duty to raise our kids in the Lord. It is our duty to not only send them to church, but that our life be a living example of what it looks like to be sold out to Jesus. Kids tend to mimic what they see. They are easily influenced. The enemy is coming after them in music, television, and school. Even church can have a not so good effect on them if you are in the wrong church. We should be doing all we can through the leading of the Holy Spirit to make sure they are being influenced by the Kingdom of God, and not the kingdom of darkness.

We should be setting them up for victory and not for failure. There are so many things that go into raising Kingdom kids. I do not believe one person can cut the bill. I believe the Father divinely places people in their lives when they need them the most. This ensures they are getting all they need and learning the lessons they need to help propel them into their future. This does not take place or get into motion without prayer. Are you ready to see your kids grow up under the admonition of the Lord?

Remember…

How did Jesus defeat Satan?

"FOR IT IS WRITTEN."

"So shall My word be that goes forth from My mouth; It shall not return to Me void, But it shall accomplish what I please, And it shall prosper in the thing for which I sent it." Isaiah 55:11 NKJV

Prayer Declaration

Father I come boldly before Your throne of grace on behalf of my children. My children are a heritage from the Lord. They are like arrows in the hand of a warrior. All my children shall be taught by the Lord, and great shall be the peace of my children. I declare my children are walking in the truth. I will not provoke my children to anger but will bring them up in the discipline and instruction of the Lord. I declare that the favor of the Lord surrounds them like a shield. I declare they have favor with teachers, friends, friends' parents, coaches, mentors, and all they are divinely connected to. Most importantly, I declare they have favor with You, their heavenly Father. I declare that all bad company is being uprooted out of their lives. For we know that bad company corrupts good character. I declare the Father is divinely placing the right, anointed men and women of God in their lives to help mature them in the things of God and for life. I declare that everything the Father has predestined them to do, they will do. I declare that no weapon formed against them shall prosper and every tongue that shall rise against them in judgment shall be condemned. I declare they will overcome every fiery dart sent against their lives by the enemy. I declare they are more than a conqueror in Christ Jesus. May perseverance arise on the inside of them. I rebuke any hindering spirits that would try to bring delay to their lives. I declare in their obedience they shall eat the good of the land, and whatever they put their hands to shall prosper. I declare they shall honor authority but stand boldly against authority that would try to have them sin against God. I declare they shall lead and not follow. I declare they hear the voice of the Lord, and the voice of a stranger they will not follow. I declare they shall retain the Good News and hide it in their heart that they may not sin against You. In Jesus' Name, amen.

Scripture References

"Behold, children are a heritage from the LORD, the fruit of the womb a reward. Like arrows in the hand of a warrior are the children of one's youth. Blessed is the man who fills his quiver with them! He shall not be put to shame when he speaks with his enemies in the gate." Psalm 127:3-5 NKJV

"All your children shall be taught by the LORD, and great shall be the peace of your children." Isaiah 54:13 NKJV

"Fathers, do not provoke your children to anger, but bring them up in the discipline and instruction of the Lord." Ephesians 6:4 NKJV

"Surely, LORD, you bless the righteous; you surround them with your favor as with a shield." Psalms 5:12 NIV

"Do not be misled: "Bad company corrupts good character." 1 Corinthians 15:33 NIV

"No weapon that is formed against thee shall prosper; and every tongue that shall rise against thee in judgment thou shalt condemn." Isaiah 54:17 KJV

"And every tongue that shall rise against thee in judgment thou shalt condemn." Ephesians 6:16 NKJV

"Yet in all these things we are more than conquerors through Him who loved us." Romans 8:37 NKJV

"If you are willing and obedient, You shall eat the good of the land." Isaiah 1:19 NKJV

"Yet they will by no means follow a stranger, but will flee from him, for they do not know the voice of strangers." John 10:5 NKJV

I have hidden your word in my heart that I might not sin against you." Psalms 119:11 NIV

For Unmerited Favor

Favor is an act of kindness beyond what is due or usual. I love that definition. You get blessed beyond what is due to you. It is the exceedingly abundant part of what you asked the Father for. He blesses you just because. Sometimes I can think on something, and He brings it to manifestation.

Every season the Father blesses me with a new pair of shoes. Sometimes one to three pairs of shoes. It depends. There were these shoes I saw online. They were extremely expensive. There is nothing wrong with expensive things. The Father wants you to have those things in His proper timing. He does not want you going out spending money for something you cannot afford at the moment. It is His job to bless you with whatever you desire when He sees fit.

Back to the shoes. So, I see these shoes, but I could not afford them. I mean I really wanted them. I said to the Lord, "One day I'll be able to buy whatever I want." Maybe a month later, I get a phone call from a friend. She found the shoes on a website for about fifteen dollars. Please understand these shoes were two hundred dollars and more. I knew this was not a fluke. I knew this was my Dad blessing me. I purchased the shoes and I absolutely love them! I could not even believe the Father. Just when I forgot all about the shoes, He blessed me with them.

Same thing happened with a pair of shoes I saw in my dream. I knew the Lord wanted me to have those shoes. Two months later, I walked right into those shoes for under twenty dollars. The same exact color I saw in the dream, and in my exact shoe size. They were the only pair. That is favor people.

It is nothing like the favor of God. Nothing like it. The favor of God can get you into places that money and your social status cannot. Favor opens doors for you in a moment of time that people have been trying to walk through for years. There is this saying, "Favor ain't fair." I agree. That is for those who are not connected to the Father.

I remember going to this Christmas party. They were

raffling off a flat screen television. I walked in the door and said, "That T.V. belong to me." Guess who walked away with the flat screen? Me.

There is a reward in being connected to the Father. Favor closes the window to lack, because in Christ nothing is lacking and nothing is missing. Favor brings you before kings and queens. Are you ready to walk in favor?

Remember...

How did Jesus defeat Satan?

"FOR IT IS WRITTEN."

"So shall My word be that goes forth from My mouth; It shall not return to Me void, But it shall accomplish what I please, And it shall prosper in the thing for which I sent it." Isaiah 55:11 NKJV

Prayer Declaration

Father, I thank You that I have favor with You and favor with man. I declare that doors are divinely opening for me because I am favored by You. Let Your favor be upon me and establish the work of my hands. For You are a sun and shield to me. You bestow favor and honor on me. No good thing will You withhold from me. I declare that I shall find favor in the Your eyesight just as Noah. I declare You are endowing me with favor and wisdom. Father show me favor and compassion in the eyesight of those who lead. Show me steadfast love and give me favor in the eyes of those who are looking in on my life. Let them see the favor of the Lord on my life that they may give their lives over to You. In Jesus' Name, amen.

Scripture References

"For you bless the righteous, O Lord; you cover him with favor as with a shield." Psalms 5:12 ESV

"Let the favor of the Lord our God be upon us, and establish the work of our hands upon us; yes, establish the work of our hands!" Psalms 90:17 ESV

"For the Lord God is a sun and shield; the Lord bestows favor and honor. No good thing does he withhold from those who walk uprightly." Psalms 84:11 ESV

"But Noah found favor in the eyes of the Lord." Genesis 6:8 ESV

"And rescued him out of all his afflictions and gave him favor and wisdom before Pharaoh, king of Egypt, who made him ruler over Egypt and over all his household." Acts 7:10 ESV

"And God gave Daniel favor and compassion in the sight of the chief of the eunuchs." Daniel 1:9 ESV

"But the Lord was with Joseph and showed him steadfast love and gave him favor in the sight of the keeper of the prison." Genesis 39:21 ESV

For Single Women in Waiting

I know all too well what it feels like to be single and waiting. I believe in transparency. I'm going to be completely honest with you. I'm going to give you the highs and lows for me. I will not over-spiritualize this.

For me, the most exhilarating moments have been growing in love with the Father every day with no interruption. I have learned how to listen and submit to Him. I have learned how to be His wife first. We walk hand-in-hand, and we are inseparable. My identity has been established in Him. I am not looking for a man to fulfill me nor complete me. Only Jesus has the ability to fill every void. I know my value now. I know I'm royal and chosen by Him. On the flip side, I do desire a husband.

Sometimes I grow a little anxious, but even in that the Father is gracious towards me.

One thing I have learned is that I can use the waiting to my advantage. I can take this time to grow, build, and mature in areas highlighted by the Holy Spirit. I can use this time to learn more about me – the things I like and the things I do not. I can learn how to sit at the feet of Jesus to glean from Him in the good and bad times of my life, or I can sit around and throw a pity party on why I'm still single and waiting. I have done them all.

I believe the Father wants to position you and your future spouse for victory. The Father wants your Kingdom marriage to resemble the Kingdom and Himself. For that to take place, there needs to be an assessment of the heart. There will be some things that need to be uprooted and worked out of both of you. I'm not saying you will be perfect when you meet your future husband, but I do believe you need to allow the Father to do whatever it is He wants to do in you.

You do not want to awake love before it is time. Allow patience to have its perfect work. Honestly, I cannot stand the word patience. On the other hand, I need to allow patience to have its perfect work in me, so what the Father began in me can be perfected. I do not want to go through unnecessary drama in marriage all because I was not willing to wait on the timing of the Lord. Are you ready to take advantage of your season of singleness?

Remember...

How did Jesus defeat Satan?

"FOR IT IS WRITTEN."

"So shall My word be that goes forth from My mouth; It shall not return to Me void, But it shall accomplish what I please, And it shall prosper in the thing for which I sent it." Isaiah 55:11 NKJV

Prayer Declaration

Father You are my strength and my shield. My heart trusts in You and I am helped. My heart greatly rejoices in You. In my waiting, teach me how to honor You and submit to You first. Father, I thank You that my identity is rooted and grounded in You alone. I know that I am loved and valued by You. I rebuke all insecurities that would make me feel like I'm not worthy or good enough. I thank You that You have come and filled every void in me. I thank You for molding me into a Proverbs 31 woman. You are grooming me to be a wife submissive to her husband.

Patience shall have its perfect work in me, so that I may be perfect and complete, not lacking anything. Anything in me that will cause delay, I ask You to expose it and uproot it. I will honor my Kingdom spouse. I will encourage my Kingdom spouse. I will use my words to build up and not tear down. I thank You for molding me into a comparable and suitable helper for my Kingdom spouse. I will not awake love before its time, but I will choose to wait on your appointed timing. I will use this time to draw closer to You. I will use this time to grow in the things of the Lord, mature, and build for the kingdom. In Jesus' Name, amen.

Scripture References

"The Lord is my strength and my shield; my heart trusted in him, and I am helped: therefore my heart greatly rejoiceth; and with my song will I praise him". Psalms 28:7 KJV

"The LORD God said, "It is not good for the man to be alone. I will make a helper suitable for him." Genesis 2:18 NIV

"Daughters of Jerusalem, I charge you: Do not arouse or awaken love until it so desires." Song of Solomon 8:4 NIV

"Rooted and built up in Him, strengthened in the faith as you were taught, and overflowing with thankfulness." Colossians 2:7 NIV

"But let patience have its perfect work, that you may be perfect and complete, lacking nothing." James 1:4 NKJV

For Waiting on the Lord

When I think about waiting, I think about my season in the wilderness. The word wait means to stay where one is or delay action until a particular time or until something else happens.

I remember going to this prophetic conference in 2019. Someone spoke these words to me, "God is about to teach you how to wait on Him." She was accurate. The following two years I was stretched in my faith in every way imaginable. Nothing came quick, and the path the Father led me to was the path of a cloud by day and fire by night. Even though that season was by far one of the most difficult seasons of my life, I grew a ton. I most definitely learned how to wait on Jesus.

Everyone needs to experience a season where you learn how to move at the heartbeat of the Holy Spirit. You do not move before or after Him. You move with Him. We now walk hand-in-hand, and I do not believe there is anything that He will not deliver me out of.

I learned to trust Him right down to the last second, because it would be the last second that He would move. Not comfortable at all, but I learned how to adapt to the way He moves. I learned to look for signs all around to encourage me to keep going. I learned He speaks in numerous ways – always giving signs of hope and always letting me know He sees me. I watched Him strengthen me in my inner man when I wanted to quit.

I stayed before Him. The waiting season took our relationship to another level. To a new place of intimacy. There is so much more to Him than the eye can see. More than you can ever fathom. He is worth waiting on.

Waiting produces character, and where some of you are going, you have no room for pride. Humility needs to be your best friend. Your season of waiting will uproot out of you anything that can hinder you from fulfilling the purpose in which you were created. It is best you allow patience to have its perfect work. If not, you will find yourself in a season longer than you have to be. The Father is faithful even in the waiting season. Are you ready to wait in expectancy?

Remember...

How did Jesus defeat Satan?

"FOR IT IS WRITTEN."

"So shall My word be that goes forth from My mouth; It shall not return to Me void, But it shall accomplish what I please, And it shall prosper in the thing for which I sent it." Isaiah 55:11 NKJV

Prayer Declaration

I will wait for the Lord and be strong. My heart will take courage knowing I do not wait in vain. I will be still before the Lord and wait patiently for Him. I will look to Him. I will wait on the God of my salvation. My God will hear me. My soul waits for Him. He is my help and my shield. My hope is in Him alone. Lead me in truth and teach me, for You are the God of my salvation. No one has heard or perceived by ear and no eye has seen a God besides You, who acts for those who wait. For You are a faithful God. A God who keeps His promises. Father, let patience have its perfect work in me so that I may be complete, lacking nothing. I will not grow weary in well doing. My strength will be renewed. I will mount on wings as eagles. I will run and not be weary. I will walk and not faint. In Jesus' Name, amen.

Scripture References

"Wait for the LORD; be strong, and let your heart take courage; wait for the LORD!" Psalms 27:14 ESV

"But they who wait for the LORD shall renew their strength; they shall mount up with wings like eagles; they shall run and not be weary; they shall walk and not faint." Isaiah 40:31 ESV

"I wait for the LORD, my soul waits, and in his word I hope" Psalms 130:5 ESV

"But as for me, I will look to the LORD; I will wait for the God of my salvation; my God will hear me." Micah 7:7 ESV

"Our soul waits for the LORD; he is our help and our shield." Psalms 33:20 ESV

"I wait for the LORD, my soul waits, and in his word I hope." Psalms 130:5 ESV

"Lead me in your truth and teach me, for you are the God of my salvation; for you I wait all the day long." Psalms 25:5 ESV

For Entrepreneurs

The Father is raising up Kingdom-focused entrepreneurs all over the world for Kingdom purposes. It is extremely important you have your ear to heaven for Kingdom business plans. You need the wisdom of God for what is to come. In the seasons ahead, it's important you let the Spirit of God lead you instead of man's logical way of doing things.

The Father is raising up millionaires and billionaires. I am aware everyone is not called to be a millionaire or billionaire, but for those that are, I'm hearing, "Much given, much will be required." I believe what the Father will have you to do will affect people all over the world in a good way. You will be the Josephs of the land. You will have the wisdom of Solomon in the marketplace.

Many will begin to invent things that bring solutions to problems that will draw in wealth. The Bible says, "Wealth and riches are in the house of the righteous." You shall obtain and have the wisdom to steward it well. Are you ready to overtake the marketplace for the Kingdom of God?

Remember...

How did Jesus defeat Satan?

"FOR IT IS WRITTEN."

"So shall My word be that goes forth from My mouth; It shall not return to Me void, But it shall accomplish what I please, And it shall prosper in the thing for which I sent it." Isaiah 55:11 NKJV

Prayer Declaration

Father, I surrender to You every business you have entrusted to me. I ask that You be the CEO of them all. Thank You that every business I put my hands to in compliance to Your will, will prosper. I declare I have the wisdom of God to steward well every business You entrust to me. I declare I will be diligent in my work so that it may lead to abundance. I will not have to toil for wealth, but I will be discerning enough to desist. I declare I will work heartily for the Lord, and not for men. Father, You make man rich and add no sorrow. I will devote myself to doing good so that my businesses may provide for urgent needs. I commit my work to You, and I trust You. Father I ask for Kingdom strategies and blueprints from heaven for my businesses. I ask that You close every door opened by the enemy, and open wide every door of opportunity from You. Give me keen discernment in my business dealings. In Jesus' Name, amen.

Scripture References

"Commit to the LORD whatever you do, and he will establish your plans." Proverbs 16:3 NIV

"Then the LORD your God will make you most prosperous in all the work of your hands and in the fruit of your womb, the young of your livestock and the crops of your land. The LORD will again delight in you and make you prosperous, just as he delighted in your ancestors." Deuteronomy 30:9 NIV

"If any of you lacks wisdom, you should ask God, who gives generously to all without finding fault, and it will be given to you." James 1:5 NIV

"I will place on his shoulder the key to the house of David; what he opens no one can shut, and what he shuts no one can open." Isaiah 22:22 NIV

"And this I pray, that your love may abound still more and more in real knowledge and all discernment, so that you may approve the things that are excellent, in order to be sincere and blameless until the day of Christ."
1 Philippians 1:9-10 NIV

For Peace

Think about a world full of chaos, or just simply look around you. Do you believe peace is attainable in the midst of the chaos? I do. The word *peace* means freedom from disturbance. Tranquility, calmness, and solitude are words that best describe peace.

Walking with Jesus has taught me no matter the circumstances, peace is available to me. There have been times when I didn't know how different urgent situations were going to play out in my life. In those times I would run to the feet of Jesus, The Prince of Peace, and pull from Him. I walked in feeling anxious and even defeated but walked away reassured that there is always hope in Him. He is the Author and Finisher of my faith. He knows my ending from the beginning, so why fret over what I have no control over? I learned to rest in Him no matter what. I am not saying I get this right every time, but what I am saying is when I feel like I am headed down a road that may lead to fear or anxiousness, I call on the Prince of Peace.

I think about Jesus and His disciples on a boat in the midst of a violent storm. Jesus told them prior to crossing over, "We are going to the other side." He did not tell them about the storm they would face as they traveled to the other side. He just simply said, "We are going to the other side."

There are times where the Father will impregnate you with an assignment, business, or ministry. He will reveal to you the starting point and the ending point but withhold the opposition you'll face to get to your ending point. He is really good about doing that. I remember a man saying, "You'll see a door, but there will be hell in the hallway to get to that door." I agree totally. I believe the Father withholds certain information to keep us from quitting before we start.

When there is a great deal of warfare we sometimes tend to think this cannot be God. Why not? Did the disciples, or anyone for that matter, who served the Lord have it easy? Not one. Every single one of them had a cross to bear.

When Joshua and Caleb crossed over into the promise land, there were giants on their land. Even though they crossed over, they still had to fight. They fought with peace knowing the land had been promised to them and they would see victory.

Going back to Jesus and the disciples on the boat. The disciples were frustrated with Jesus because He was asleep while they were awake in fear of the storm. Jesus simply arose and said, "Peace be still." They wondered who is this Man that even the winds obey.

I have Good News. You have the same authority Jesus has. The same way Jesus rebuked the storm, you have the ability to rebuke the storm in your life. Are you ready to live from a place of peace?

Remember...

How did Jesus defeat Satan?

"FOR IT IS WRITTEN."

"So shall My word be that goes forth from My mouth; It shall not return to Me void, But it shall accomplish what I please, And it shall prosper in the thing for which I sent it." Isaiah 55:11 NKJV

Prayer Declaration

I declare that grace, mercy, and peace will be with me from the Prince of Peace, Jesus Christ. May mercy and peace be multiplied unto me and may the peace of Christ rule in my heart. The peace of God which surpasses all understanding, will guard my heart and my mind in Christ Jesus. I shall live from a place of righteousness, peace, and joy in the Holy Spirit. May the God of hope fill me with all joy and peace believing that the power of the Holy Spirit will enable me to abound in hope. Father You said, "Peace I leave with you, My peace I give to you. Not as the world gives do I give to you." I receive Your peace today. My heart will not be troubled, and I will not be afraid. Long life is in my right hand. In my left hand are riches and honor. My ways are pleasant, and my paths are peace. I am a tree of life to those who lay hold of me. Those who hold me fast are called blessed. In Jesus' Name, amen.

Scripture References

"Long life is in her right hand; in her left hand are riches and honor. Her ways are ways of pleasantness, and all her paths are peace. She is a tree of life to those who lay hold of her; those who hold her fast are called blessed." Proverbs 3:16-18 NIV

"Peace I leave with you; my peace I give to you. Not as the world gives do I give to you. Let not your hearts be troubled, neither let them be afraid." John 14:27 NIV

"May the God of hope fill you with all joy and peace in believing, so that by the power of the Holy Spirit you may abound in hope." Romans 15:13 NIV

"For the kingdom of God is not a matter of eating and drinking but of righteousness and peace and joy in the Holy Spirit." Romans 14:17 NIV

"And the peace of God, which surpasses all understanding, will guard your hearts and your minds in Christ Jesus." Philippians 4:7 NIV

"And let the peace of Christ rule in your hearts, to which indeed you were called in one body. And be thankful." Colossians 3:15 NIV

"Now may the Lord of peace himself give you peace at all times in every way. The Lord be with you all." 2 Thessalonians 3:16 NIV

For Keen Discernment

The word *keen* means highly developed. Sharp and clear are words that best describe keen. The word *discern* means to distinguish someone or something with difficulty by sight or with the other senses. Perceive, make out, detect, recognize, notice, observe, distinguish, differentiate, and identify are all words that best describe discern. I love the synonyms that breaks down the word discern.

As we move forward towards the end times, we need keen discernment. We need to be sharp and clear in our discernment so we can recognize truth. We need to be able to discern evil from good. In today's culture we call evil good and good evil. This is not only in the world, but also in the church. We have opened the door and allowed imposters in. They talk like us, preach like us, sing just as good as us, but their heart is far from God. They have no anointing to break the yoke of bondage off anyone. It seems that most are having a hard time in distinguishing between a gift and an anointing. We don't need words of fluff with charisma wrapped around them. We need words that carry authority and weight in the spiritual realm. We need to know the difference. I need to know if I am talking to a follower of Jesus Christ or an imposter.

Every open door is not a God-opened door. You need to be able to discern the difference. Is this divine or is this a trap? Spend time with the Lord regularly and intentionally so that your discernment can heighten. Are you ready for your discernment to heighten?

Remember…

How did Jesus defeat Satan?

"FOR IT IS WRITTEN."

"So shall My word be that goes forth from My mouth; It shall not return to Me void, But it shall accomplish what I please, And it shall prosper in the thing for which I sent it." Isaiah 55:11 NKJV

Prayer Declaration

I declare that I will be able to distinguish good from evil because my discernment will heighten with trained constant practice and well spent time with Jesus. I declare that love will abound in me more and more, with knowledge and all discernment. In this I will be able to approve what is excellent, and so be pure and blameless for the day of Christ. For the Word of God is alive and active in my life and because of that I will be able to discern the thoughts and intentions of others as well as myself. I declare I have clear and sharp discernment. I declare I will make out, perceive, recognize, detect, and identify good from evil. I declare I will not believe every spirit, but I will test the spirit to see whether they are from God. In Jesus' Name, amen.

Scripture References

"Beloved, do not believe every spirit, but test the spirits to see whether they are from God, for many false prophets have gone out into the world." 1 John 4:1 ESV

"But solid food is for the mature, for those who have their

powers of discernment trained by constant practice to distinguish good from evil." Hebrews 5:14 ESV

"And it is my prayer that your love may abound more and more, with knowledge and all discernment, so that you may approve what is excellent, and so be pure and blameless for the day of Christ." Philippians 1:9-10 ESV

"For the word of God is living and active, sharper than any two-edged sword, piercing to the division of soul and of spirit, of joints and of marrow, and discerning the thoughts and intentions of the heart." Hebrews 4:12 ESV

"Give your servant therefore an understanding mind to govern your people, that I may discern between good and evil, for who is able to govern this your great people?" 1 King 3:9 ESV

For Declaring the Blood of Jesus

I remember having a dream where I told this group of people, "When the doctor said she couldn't do anything for me, the blood of Jesus healed me." I then said, "There is power in the blood of Jesus."

The worst thing we can do is minimize the blood of Jesus. Do you know there is power in what Jesus did on the cross for you and me? Do you know there is power in the finished work of the cross? Please hear me… THERE IS POWER IN THE BLOOD OF JESUS!

Revelation 12:11 says, "And they overcame him by the blood of the Lamb and by the word of their testimony, and they did not love their lives to the death."

Who is him? Satan. It is through Jesus' blood we have

victory. It is through the blood of Jesus that we are able to trample on the lion and adder. It is through the blood of Jesus that we are able to escape premature death. It is through the blood of Jesus that we get the chance to live in eternity with the Father. Only by His blood do we stand today in our right mind.

There is this old Baptist hymn I love to sing. "What can wash away my sin? Nothing but the blood of Jesus. What can make me whole again? Nothing but the blood of Jesus." There is power in the blood! Are you ready to apply the blood of Jesus to your life?

Remember…

How did Jesus defeat Satan?

"FOR IT IS WRITTEN."

"So shall My word be that goes forth from My mouth; It shall not return to Me void, But it shall accomplish what I please, And it shall prosper in the thing for which I sent it." Isaiah 55:11 NKJV

Prayer Declaration

Father, thank You for the blood of Jesus. Oh, how precious is the flow. May the blood of Jesus flow through every part of my being, cleansing me of all impurities, sickness, infections, and diseases. May it cleanse away all sin, and I ask that You create in me a clean heart and a righteous spirit. Because of Your blood, I have been redeemed. I have been redeemed from the curse of the law because You, Jesus, became the curse for me. I plead Your blood over my household for protection from premature death. May sickness, disease, and all plagues pass over my household because of Your blood. I plead Your blood over my mind, and I declare I have the mind of Christ. Your blood has washed me and made me white as snow. Your blood shall be on me and my children. Thank You for Your sacrifice. Thank You for Your blood. In Jesus' Name, amen.

Scripture References

"In Him we have redemption through His blood, the forgiveness of our trespasses, according to the riches of His grace." Ephesians 1:7 NASB

"And all the people said, "His blood shall be on us and on our children!" Matthew 27:25 NASB

"But if we walk in the light, as he is in the light, we have fellowship with one another, and the blood of Jesus his Son cleanses us from all sin." 1 John 1:7 NIV

"And they have conquered him by the blood of the Lamb and by the word of their testimony, for they loved not their lives even unto death." Revelation 12:11 NIV

"The blood shall be a sign for you on the houses where you live; and when I see the blood I will pass over you, and no plague will befall you to destroy you when I strike the land of Egypt." Exodus 12:13 NASB

For the Consuming Fire of God to Overtake You

Some people may be afraid and running from the fire of God. However, I am not. I need the fire of God to come and burn away anything about me that does not look like Him. Here I am Father, consume me. Hebrews 12:29 says, "God is a consuming fire." Who wouldn't want to be consumed by the Father?

Not only do I see God's fire as something that purifies, but I also see it as something that endows you with power. I think about the disciples in the Upper Room waiting on the promised Helper, the Holy Spirit.

In Matthew 3:11 NIV John says, "I baptize you with water for repentance, but He who is coming after me is mightier than I, whose sandals I am not worthy to carry. He will baptize you with the Holy Spirit and fire." John said, "He will baptize you with the Holy Spirit and FIRE." This is not something to shun upon, but rather something to welcome. Here, two baptisms are acknowledged. One for repentance of sin by way of water, and the other for power by way of fire.

Acts 2:1-4 NIV says, "When the day of Pentecost came, they were all together in one place. Suddenly a sound like the blowing of a violent wind came from heaven and filled the whole house where they were sitting. They saw what seemed to be tongues of fire that separated and came to rest on each of them. All of them were filled with the Holy Spirit and began to speak in other tongues as the Spirit enabled them."

When the fire of God hit them, they were able to do what they were not able to do at first. I cannot speak for anyone else, but I am choosing to run to the fire and not away from the fire. Are you ready for the all-consuming fire of God?

Remember…

How did Jesus defeat Satan?

"FOR IT IS WRITTEN."

"So shall My word be that goes forth from My mouth; It shall not return to Me void, But it shall accomplish what I please, And it shall prosper in the thing for which I sent it." Isaiah 55:11 NKJV

Prayer Declaration

Father overtake me with Your all-consuming fire. Burn away anything in me that does not glorify You. Purify me, oh God. Refine me in Your refiner's fire that I may come out pure as gold. Fill me with Your Holy Spirit and baptize me in the fire of the Holy Ghost that I may receive power to enable me to go throughout the world and spread the Gospel of Jesus Christ. In Jesus' Name, amen.

Scripture References

"God is a consuming fire." Hebrews 12:29 NIV

"These have come so that the proven genuineness of your faith of greater worth than gold, which perishes even though refined by fire may result in praise, glory and honor when Jesus Christ is revealed." 1 Peter 1:7 NIV

"They saw what seemed to be tongues of fire that separated and came to rest on each of them. All of them were filled with the Holy Spirit and began to speak in other tongues as the Spirit enabled them." Acts 2:3-4 NIV

"But you will receive power when the Holy Spirit has come upon you; and you shall be My witnesses both in Jerusalem, and in all Judea and Samaria, and even to the remotest part of the earth." Acts 1:8 NASB

Other books by Carlnika Hooks:

To receive email updates, read blogs, or purchase resources, please visit **www.carlnikahooks.com**.

All eBooks can be found on carlnikahooks.com and all paperbacks can be found on amazon.com.

Please follow Carlnika Hooks and her ministries on social media at:

Facebook: Carlnika Hooks

Instagram: @carlnikahooks

Facebook: The Who Is She Affect

INSTAGRAM: @thewhoissheaffect

www.ingramcontent.com/pod-product-compliance
Lightning Source LLC
Chambersburg PA
CBHW060202050426
42446CB00013B/2961